Technology For All

Wi-Fi
Around the World

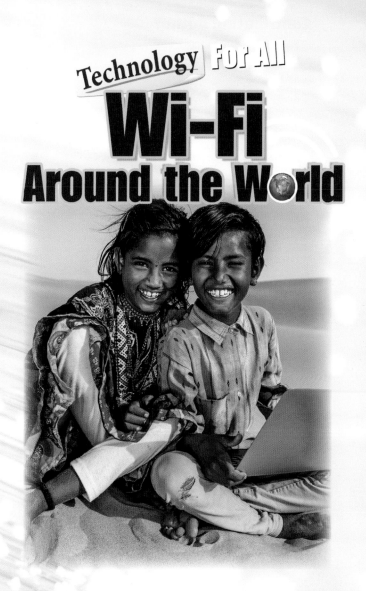

David Bjerklie

Contributing Author

Timothy Pasch, Ph.D.
University of North Dakota

Publishing Credits

Rachelle Cracchiolo, M.S.Ed., *Publisher*
Conni Medina, M.A.Ed., *Managing Editor*
Nika Fabienke, Ed.D., *Series Developer*
June Kikuchi, *Content Director*
John Leach, *Assistant Editor*
Kevin Pham, *Graphic Designer*

TIME For Kids and the TIME For Kids logo are registered trademarks of TIME Inc. Used under license.

Image Credits: pp.4–5 Sergey Nivens/Alamy Stock Photo; p.10 Frederic Legrand - COMEO/Shutterstock.com; pp.12–13, 20–21 Illustrations by Timothy J. Pasch; pp.14–15 Galaxiid/Alamy Stock Photo; pp.18–19 CB2/ZOB/Supplied by WENN.com/Newscom; pp.22–23 Hero Images Inc./Alamy Stock Photo; all other images from iStock and/or Shutterstock.

All companies and products mentioned in this book are registered trademarks of their respective owners or developers and are used in this book strictly for editorial purposes; no commercial claim to their use is made by the author or the publisher.

Library of Congress Cataloging-in-Publication Data

Names: Bjerklie, David, author. | Pasch, Timothy, author.
Title: Technology for all : Wi-Fi around the world / David Bjerklie ; contributing author, Timothy Pasch, Ph.D.
Description: Huntington Beach, CA : Teacher Created Materials, [2018] | Includes index. | Audience: K to grade 3.
Identifiers: LCCN 2017013464 (print) | LCCN 2017030994 (ebook) | ISBN 9781425853488 (eBook) | ISBN 9781425849740 (paperback)
Subjects: LCSH: Wireless communication systems—Juvenile literature.
Classification: LCC TK5103.2 (ebook) | LCC TK5103.2 .B52 2018 (print) | DDC 004.6/8—dc23
LC record available at https://lccn.loc.gov/2017013464

Teacher Created Materials
5301 Oceanus Drive
Huntington Beach, CA 92649-1030
http://www.tcmpub.com
ISBN 978-1-4258-4974-0
© 2018 Teacher Created Materials, Inc.

Table of Contents

Looking to Connect

Imagine you are sitting in class. Are you in the front row? Or do you like to sit in the back? School is almost over for the day. Your teacher gives the class a homework assignment. You will need to use a computer. And the homework is due tomorrow morning.

Your heart sinks because you know you will not be able to finish it. You understand the homework, and you want to do a good job. But you will not be able to do the work because you can't connect to the **Internet** from your home.

Open for Use

The Internet first came to public use in the early 1990s. Since then, it has changed the way many students do homework.

Left Behind

Millions of children in the United States cannot connect to the Internet. In parts of Africa and Asia (see map above), the numbers are also high. Some families do not know what the Internet is. Some cannot afford to connect. And others live in areas that are hard to reach.

Sending Signals

It is easy to send messages today. People can use a telephone or a computer. These inventions took a long time and a lot of hard work to create. But the effort was worth it. Now, communication moves much faster.

Many years ago, people found a way to send messages through wires. This was called the *telegraph*. The first telephones also used wires.

Inventors then found a way to send messages through the air. The first device to do this was the radio. Then came the television. Now, images can also be sent. We still use wires and airwaves to send messages.

Wires and Waves

We live in a world of **networks**. They carry messages, music, voices, and video. We can use networks to learn about the world.

A woman uses a telegraph to send a message.

Before Text Messaging

Telegrams are similar to text messages. But they were written in a special shorthand code. The messages traveled through wires. They were the fastest way to send messages when they were invented in 1844.

Technology gets better all the time. Even wires get better. We now have wires called **high-speed cables**. These bring the Internet to towns and cities. Special equipment also lets people connect to the Internet without wires. This is called Wi-Fi.

People use Wi-Fi at home. They also use it in restaurants and coffee shops. They can even use it on trains and planes. That means more people can use the Internet. They use it to read and to learn. They also use it to listen to music and to watch videos.

Around the World

More than three billion people in the world use the Internet. Yet there are still more than four billion who are not connected! But this number is slowly changing.

Top Five

These five countries have the most people connected to the Internet.

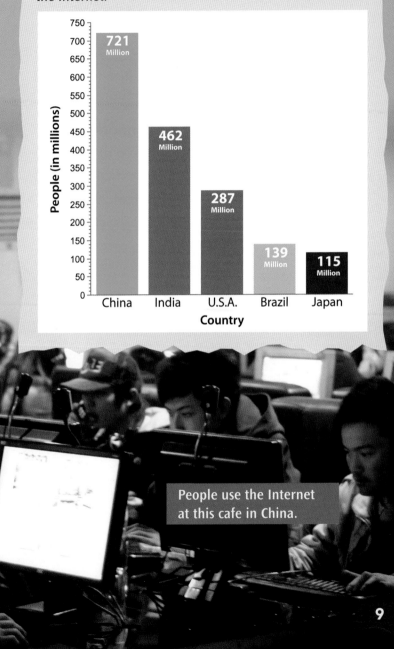

People use the Internet at this cafe in China.

Making Contact

The Internet makes the world feel smaller. It makes it easy for people to connect. You can send a message to a friend in your town. Or you can send messages to friends all over the world.

More people than ever are connected to the Internet. But many people still live in places that are too hard to reach by high-speed cable. This can make them feel cut off from the rest of the world. The kids who live in Arviat (ahr-vee-AHT) in the **Arctic** often feel this way.

Global Village

"The Internet is becoming the town square for the global village of tomorrow."

—Bill Gates, founder of Microsoft

At Home in the North

Arviat is a town on the Hudson Bay in a part of Canada called Nunavut (NOO-nuh-vuht). It is in the Arctic. It is home to the Inuit people. They have lived there for thousands of years.

Melville I.

Lancaster Sound

Davis Strait

Viscount Melville Sound

Amundsen Gulf

Victoria I.

M'Clintoch Channel

Baffin Island

Gulf of Boothia

Owen Maud Gulf

NORTHWEST TERRITORIES

Ungava Bay

Great Slave Lake

Dubawnt

 Arviat

Hudson Bay

QUÉBEC

Lake Athabasca

Athabasca

Nelson

Severn

James Bay

La Grande Rivière

ALBERTA

SASKATCHEWAN

N. Saskatchewan

Saskatchewan

MANITOBA

Lake Winnipeg

ONTARIO

Lake Winnipegosis

Albany

Children in Arviat want to reach out. They want to connect to the rest of the world. To do this, they make videos about their lives and traditions. They film one another hunting. They film themselves fishing. They film polar bears, too. They also make videos about their challenges.

But to share more videos, they need faster Internet connections. New technology might be able to help. It will let them share their work with the world. And they will be able to see how other people live.

Seeing the Sights

The Internet lets people learn about places they will never visit. People all over the world can share their stories and their homes online. You can see rain forests, deserts, and faraway cities!

Arctic Conditions

What is it like in Arviat? In the Arctic, the days are very long during the summer. The nights are very long during the winter. It is also very cold in the winter. There are strong winds and blizzards!

Students in Arviat plan their next video.

Sharing Is Caring

People in Arviat have a lot of stories to tell about their lives. Here are some of the stories they want to share with you.

"I want to show people how we dry **caribou** meat and collect wild geese eggs."

—Eva Suluk

"I want to tell kids about **inukshuks**. And how they are made."

—Huluk Suluk

"I want to teach people about Inuit **throat singing**. It's hard. I learned when I was young."

—Nuatie Aggark

"I want to teach people about hope. What hope means to me."

—Ethan Tassiuk

A Voice for All

The United Nations (UN) was formed in 1945. It helps countries work together. The UN protects **human rights** for people around the world. The UN wants all countries to connect to the Internet. That way, people can reach out to others online.

A local woman holds a traditional tool used by the Inuit.

Innovative Ideas

Telephones once needed wires to work. Computers needed wires to connect to the Internet. Your parents or grandparents remember this time. But things have changed. Today, these devices do not always need wires. They use Wi-Fi. For Wi-Fi to work, it needs to connect to larger networks. High-speed cables make this possible.

These larger networks are like roads that connect cities. If you have a fast connection, then the road near you has many lanes. Information, like the cars on the road, moves very fast.

If the larger networks are the roads, then Wi-Fi is like the driveway to each home. To connect, we need both.

Underwater Cable

In 1858, people put a telegraph cable on the ocean floor. This cable connected Ireland and Canada. Cables like this are very strong. But they can be damaged. Fishing **trawlers** have damaged cables. Earthquakes can harm cables, too. Some cables have been bitten by sharks!

Internet High and Low

Connections are everywhere—from the ocean floor to the sky. Satellites **orbit** Earth and beam the Internet around the world.

Balloons

Inventors are developing new ways to deliver Internet service. Google® is a famous company that started as a search engine. It is trying to find ways for more people to connect. It is using large balloons to create a network. The balloons use **lasers** to beam the Internet. Many balloons are needed to make the balloon network work.

The balloons need to float for a long time. At first, the balloons could stay up in the air for only a week. But now they can float for almost 200 days. That is more than six months! The balloons fly more than 11 miles (18 kilometers) in the air, which is much higher than airplanes.

More Than Hot Air

Balloons come in many sizes. Some balloons are strong enough to carry people. These are called hot-air balloons. People can go for a ride in a basket hanging from one of these big balloons.

Sky High

The network balloons are filled with **helium** to make them lighter than air. They are each 39 feet (12 meters) tall and 49 feet (15 meters) wide. It is hard to keep the balloons in one place. The balloons ride wind currents.

Drones

Facebook™ is another company that wants to create a network in the sky. It uses planes without pilots. These planes are called drones. They are flown by remote control. The project is called Aquila (uh-KEE-luh), which is the **Latin** word for *eagle*. The drones use solar power. They fly more than 10 miles (16 kilometers) high. That is above all the weather that occurs on Earth.

Most drones are very small. But these drones are unusually large. They measure 141 feet (43 meters) from the tip of one wing to the tip of the other. The drones weigh 1,000 pounds (454 kilograms). That is less than the lightest car.

Mini Satellites

Another way to create a network is to use small satellites. Thousands of them would be launched into space. Each satellite would be the size of a toaster. Imagine a bunch of toasters floating in space! Could they provide Internet connection? Yes, if there are enough of them.

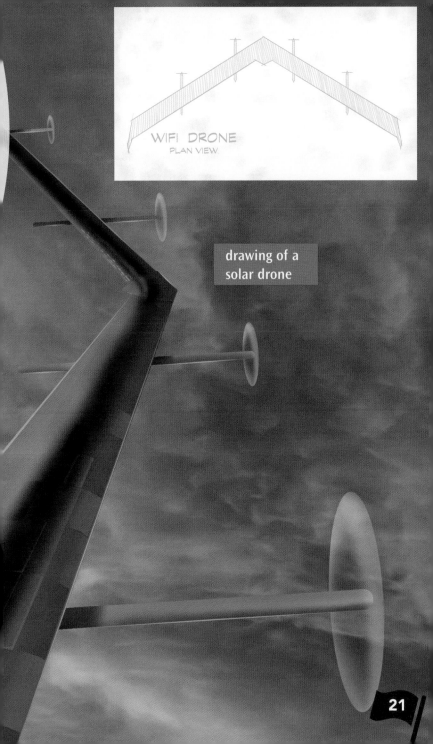

WIFI DRONE
PLAN VIEW

drawing of a
solar drone

Staying Grounded

There are many ideas about how to bring the Internet to people. Not all of the ideas are up in the air. There are also many ideas for solutions on the ground. Here is one example. In many places, school buses provide Wi-Fi. This helps kids do homework on their way to and from school. Some of the same buses help after school, too. How? At night, the buses park in neighborhoods without Internet. That means kids can connect from home, too.

Cruising Wi-Fi

Remote areas of Australia are not connected to the Internet. People there are trying to use **rugged** cars equipped with Wi-Fi. The cars create a moving network. This can help in an emergency. The cars are being tested as a message system. This idea might work in other areas, too.

Connected Trains

People want to use the Internet when they travel. Millions of people travel by train. Many companies are trying to solve this problem. They are working together. They want to provide free Wi-Fi on trains.

The Power of Connection

The Internet helps people in many ways. It gives them information. This helps people do their jobs. It helps students with schoolwork.

It also helps in other ways. What if you live far away from any city? You are sick and need help. There are no hospitals close by. What can you do?

Being able to connect to the Internet makes a big difference. It gives people access to medical information. It even allows them to talk with doctors and nurses hundreds of miles away.

Future Farming

How dry are the fields? Are bugs eating the crops? What will the weather be next week? All this information can be collected and shared with farmers over the Internet.

What Is Next?

People all over the world access the Internet. But most of it is written in English. Is this a problem? Some people think so. They worry that English will push out other languages.

One way to stop this is to make sure many languages are used online. This will help keep these other cultures and languages alive. This way, more people can use their own languages. They can learn about different places. They can learn about different cultures. Being connected doesn't have to make us all the same.

Catching Up

Researchers look at which languages are used the most on the Internet. They looked at the top 10 million websites. They found that more than half of the sites use English. Russian is in second place. It is used on about 6 out of 100 sites.

How Do You Say It?

One way the Internet can speak someone's language is by using translators. They can turn words in one language into another. Have you ever used one?

Glossary

Arctic—northernmost part of the world

caribou—species of North American reindeer

helium—a gas lighter than air, used to make balloons float

high-speed cables—special wires that can carry information

human rights—basic rights and freedoms

Internet—global network connecting millions of computers

inukshuks (ih-NOOK-shooks)—man-made stone markers made for communication and orientation

lasers—intense beams of focused light

Latin—language of ancient Rome and its empire

networks—systems with connected parts

orbit—to circle around

rugged—strongly built

throat singing—traditional form of singing and musical performance

trawlers—fishing boats that drag heavy nets across the bottom of the sea

Index

Check It Out!

Books

Anniss, Matt. 2014. *How Does Wi-Fi Work?*
    Gareth Stevens Publishing.

Websites

EveryoneOn. everyoneon.org.

Office of Educational Technology. *ConnectED*.
    www.tech.ed.gov/connected/.

Project Loon. x.company/loon/.

Articles

Hempel, Jessi. "Inside Facebook's
    Ambitious Plan to Connect the Whole
    World." www.wired.com/2016 /01/
    facebook-zuckerberg-internet-org/.

Kang, Cecilia. "Bridging a Digital Divide That
    Leaves Schoolchildren Behind." www.nytimes.
    com/2016/02/23/technology/fcc-internet-access-
    school.html.

Try It!

Does your grandmother, grandfather, or another older relative use the Internet? If so, ask what he or she uses it for. If not, help him or her find reasons to connect. In what ways can the Internet be useful to older people? In what ways do you use the Internet differently from them?

Be a reporter, and record the answers in a notebook. Encourage friends to do the same. Then, compare your findings!

About the Authors

David Bjerklie studied biology and anthropology at the University of North Dakota and spent three months on a tiny island studying spotted sandpipers. He has written about science, medicine, technology, and the environment for *TIME*, *TIME FOR KIDS*, and *TIME Books*. He is the author of books for children and young adults. In 2014, he traveled to Antarctica as a National Science Foundation media fellow.

Timothy Pasch, Ph.D., (co-author of the "Making Contact" chapter) is a professor of digital communication at the University of North Dakota. He studies the impact of technology on languages and cultures. He travels to the Arctic to help remote communities connect online. Dr. Pasch speaks English, French, and Japanese. He is still learning the Inuit language, Inuktitut, which he says is the most challenging of all!